THUNDERBIRD INN

THUNDERBIRD INN

Collin
CALLAHAN

Printed in the United States of America

ISBN: 978-1-7336020-8-2

Published by Conduit Books & Ephemera
788 Osceola Avenue
Saint Paul, Minnesota 55105
www.conduit.org

Book design by Scott Bruno/b graphic design

Distributed by Small Press Distribution
www.spdbooks.org

Cover images: Carol M. Highsmith: *The Vintage Hacienda Motel,* 2020; *A very old, very deteriorated motel sign,* 2020; *Motel in Morehead, Kentucky,* 2020; *Rule Irwin outside a cottage in Moorcroft, Wyoming,* 2015. All photos courtesy of the Library of Congress.

CONTENTS

III.

IV.

for

LINDSEY

I

America Votes for the Talking Machine

I walk my burrito around
the outlet mall.

The suburban air is antiseptic
and cinnamon. Corporate music

splurges from a loudspeaker
in the bullseye of the food court.

I observe snack time traffic
from the elevated vantage

of a plastic horse while round children
press their foreheads against the sneezeguard

of a pretzel kiosk. The saliva
puddle at their feet widens

into a small pond. The mannequins
could be any of us.

Dear Corporation

Richard and I knife the moonrocks
into separate piles
on a mattress hidden in the skimp forest outline
of an industrial park.
They crackle like rat skulls
in the blades of a lawnmower.
Richard squiggles warmblood
horses on a napkin
as I rock back and forth like a machine
full of wet clothes.
Moths powder the handrails of gaunt stairwells.
This light has the quality
of a midwestern hospital.
Nitrous canisters lie about.
I think about submarine warfare
and those balloons in the dead girl's backyard.
The electrical plant is pink thunder.
I tuck the aluminum foil into my breast pocket
like a beautiful child.

Horizontal Tuxedo

She left me her address
in wet hair on the shower wall.
I begin drawing lobster
weddings—a planktonic ring bearer and coral
girl shadowing the crustaceous couple
down the sea-cathedral's center aisle,
claws of relatives clacking in approval.
When I run out of pencils, I origami
my favorite ceremony into a fishing boat
and leave for the post office.
The sky is a moldy orange. Dark birds
circle my head like musical
chairs. At each telephone pole, I pause
to run my fingers across
rusted staple constellations
left over from lost dog signs.

Deerfield Crossing

Sheet lightning pulses like blood
vessels in the sky above the post office.

It is Sunday empty. I caress the edges
of failed delivery in my pocket

and continue on the acid-
rain pocked sidewalk to the station.

Down the block, a dog fights his leash
toward the smell of angel hair

and meatballs
escaping from a kitchen window.

Television sets and crickets coalesce
with the steady hum of residential air

conditioning units. The syncopated eyes
of wind turbines blink red in the distance.

Families fold together
their fingers in prayer.

When the thunder claps

like an infomercial
the streetlamps come on

all at once.

Salt & Pepper Diner

Pollen shadows swim
in a polygon of sunlight

on the table between Nancy and I.
She presses her rhubarb lips

to a folded cloth napkin.
Her eyes bring to mind

prison mirrors.
While I am forking

my self-portrait in egg yolk, she says,
I'll quit smoking cigarettes

when Jesus takes me home.
A horseshoe of waitstaff

forms for a nearby birthday.
Nancy hums along

as I search her purse for antihistamines.
The floor is a chessboard.

Outside, the cars shine like salmon
in the convenience store parking lot.

Thunderbird Inn

The desk lady repeats
herself like a telephone menu

as I diagram the fire
exits and security cameras.

The motel pool is cerulean.
The hot tub—out of order.

Richard squints in the reverse image
of himself. *A little more.*
I scissor his rattail

and sponge his neck.
My tongue is a garden slug.
We button our thrifted florals.

At a soft banana,
I flick
cards as Richard twiddles

the antennas
like a forklift operator.

He twists biblical spliffs.
Curtains warble in the television light.

Each siren is a doom spiral.
The highway exhales like a horse.

In the Arms of a Peachleaf Willow off I-55

a flittering of rust-
bellied birds chirp like smoke alarms
low on battery.

From tendrils of shade,
I sketch a ribbon
snake unwinding on a stone,

as airplane left lines
fade like denim
into the darkening sky.

A semi lies—jackknifed—
in the median of the interstate.
The air is thick with diesel.

Radio personalities spill
like lukewarm coffee
out of passing car windows.

If I listen close,
I can almost hear
a freckle of a man

on the shoulder of Exit 13—
shaking
his styrofoam cup
tambourine.

Songs Build Little Rooms in Time

for DB

The smallest, even.
And I find you there, cowlicked

in a scrawl of menthol.
I inch along a shelf of caricatures

while the air conditioner sputters
onward like a tugboat

in emergency water.
We talk of radio towers

and poached eggs
and lakeshore traffic

and not the careful white triangle
on the end table.

I steady the ceiling fan
with a folded postcard as you

hold the rotary telephone
in your lap like a shiny dog.

The dial is a Ferris wheel.
I wait for you to make the call.

Leftovers

Richard and I nurse tall boys
in the alley behind Pizza Kastle.
Coin operated machines tumble wet

clothes in nearby basements
as bluegrass hobbles out of a portable radio
like a sun-drenched grandfather.

I unzip at the dumpster.
Invisible helicopters hummingbird
overhead. Richard shakes out

the abysmal tip jar.
Gasoline rainbows in pothole water.
I have been sleeping

in a closet above Planet Hollywood.
A white mouse lives inside the wall.
I call him Leonard.

He gnaws garlic knots,
tail dangling
off the corner of the mattress.

I Hummed Her Address Until It Existed in Front of Me

I.

A freshly hatched
chicken-yellow bungalow
pinched between high rises.
Fists of ivy cling to the siding
like a boy afraid of losing his mother
in a crowded supermarket.
I want so much
to be invited inside
for chamomile tea.
To discuss ceiling fans
and the migratorial implications
of wind farming.
To pick up a childhood
photograph from the fireplace mantel
I too was a werewolf
once on Halloween.
It is too early.
Even the postman still home
spooning sugar into his medium roast.
A distant police siren
stirs me toward doughnuts.
The sycamore in her yard
I note:
ideal for climbing.

II.

She gets home from work around 5:30
and asks, "How long have you been in that tree?"
I respond by continuing to focus all energy
on my inner-goldfinch.
I have been perching
for this bird-acting gig I picked up
a few years ago.
My calves are watermelons.
They call it method acting.

Richard and I Split the Last of It

in the wooden skeleton
of a saltbox home.

We came up
slow—knee to knee
on sawdust carpet

in the master bathtub.
The night held
rectangles above us.

Each star a stray nail
in an unkempt toolbox.
My palms grew unfamiliar

as banana spiders
parachuted
limply earthward.

To distract from a potential
downward spiral
Richard described his favorite

tree—a willow across
the tracks from a midwestern storefront
just outside Giant City. *"Last year*

they had a festival for the solar eclipse.
The willow was in the path of totality."
A strange pressure unsnarled

like a milk snake
inside my eyelid

while Richard knifed his birthday
into the frame of a door.

I hummed. And I hummed
in a cavity between countertops.
Look Richard. Look.

I am the refrigerator.

II

Candlelight Motel

I point the taxi cab
toward the gravel swamp just past
a corrugated shed pregnant with hipsters
and fuzz rock.
The cardboard tree twizzles
as Richard and I exit the town car.
The rain is a plastic robot
falling down stairs.
A metalhead joysticks his chair
to the ice machine—
straw jittering in his breast pocket
like a flightless bird.
Richard knuckles the faded door.
A doodle squats in the communal garden
near a giant sunflower.
Bryan, our plug, waves us in.
Offers the refrigerator.
Each wall is a mess of cuckoo clocks.
The couch smells like liver failure.
Richard lays the Polaroids
on the table like baseball cards.
A mannequin leans against the sliding
glass. The newscast is seagull clatter.
Bryan asks if he can
suck my toes.
What's the big deal, boy?
I can't even get hard.

Stardust Bowl

Richard snorts more horse tranquilizer
in the X-mart parking lot.
I spray black paint on a pellet gun.
Meteors shrivel in the night.

The league thins
like neon-lit scalp hair
as we jaw our way toward the door.
The drip is a slaughter

of spotted piglets
lowered into the scalding tank
one by one.
My head is a hillside
of meat hooks.

The gameroom blinks like a satellite.
A bowling pin dinosaur
is decimated by a strike.
Richard's fingernails are foxfires

in the cosmic light.
The alley manager sprinkles antifungal
on a row of shoe rentals.
The nacho machine vomits gold.

Richard walks to the counter
like a car accident.
The spiral of an electric stovetop
in each of his palms.

Milk Tooth

The postman blinks at the television
like a sedated elephant.
An explosion of dark sparrows

spiral above the water tower.
The bathroom mirror is a steamboat
engine. Glue-trapped, a mouse

gnaws its pink leg
beneath the refrigerator.

I test out the musicality of various
silverware. Spoon. Cheese grater.

The crickets fizzle, radios burble.
Horseless, we conspire.

The sky is purple
and enormous. Look at me.
Tell me I matter.

Server Appreciation Day

I sew my wisdom
teeth into the open mouth

of a plush horse. A gift for the giant
woman who tends the tiki bar

where blowfish hang like mistletoe.
Her freckles a moonlit field

of Casa Blanca lilies. After I tie off
the final stitch—shear the excess—

I remove the rubber
thimble from my thumb

and house the needle
in a tomato pincushion.

Coffin Rehearsal

I.

Richard sucks my backpack tube
like a fetus
as we shadow the mechanical tracks
of a bobcat

toward the silo.
A realtor grins in each yard.
The rainfall is peach stubble.
Richard's jaw shifts

like a grandfather clock
as warblers lilt in dwarf pines
on the shoreline
of an artificial pond.

I eyeball the ratio of gasoline
to engine oil.
Richard waterproofs
a shoebox time capsule.

The padlock opens like a field of legs.
I take ten steps
in the excavation light.
Pull the choke.

II.

The aquascape specialist lifts a bullet
to his left nostril.
The koi shipment sloshes about.

III.

I build a terrarium the exact dimensions
of my childhood closet.

Pace figure eights
like a zoo leopard

in the cabin of warm air.
Snails clutch the ceiling.

I glue a scarecrow
of rabbit bones together.

Wilson Park

The giant woman zips along
on a pair of rollerskates.
If only, by chance, I was nearby
the moment her ankle snapped

like a stick of celery
and I spotted her in the grass
beneath a poplar tree

I would set this white pill on her tongue.
A lightbulb
in a wet cave.

/

I fish her curls from the drain.
I shave her legs.
I say yes. Of course. Okay.

/

The ice cream truck is turning
in our direction.
On a portable television

bombs fall. We cheer
for the little black airplanes.

In the Tunnel

underneath Ninety-fifth Street
I drop a few dead presidents
into the overturned fedora

of a man with the face of a baby
tattooed on his forearm.

He performs on a stage
of overturned milk crates.
Banjo chords buffet the walls

like pigeons in a glass suitcase.
A voice in the ceiling

apologizes for maintenance-related
issues, so I follow people with ears

plugged into their telephones
toward stainless turnstiles.

Upstairs, uniforms on horses
patrol the lunch hour.

My backpack is a dartboard.
I tip my cap.

Rumor of a Warrant

Children float around Richard
and I like bandages.
The airplane noise is wet chalk.

The Astrovan sits in front of eleven,
just as the barflies predicted.
A man in spiked leather pours charcoal
into a metal chimney
and slaps hamburgers onto a paper plate.

They call me Big Hands. The pleasure
is all yours.
I deal out a sixer of Icehouse—
the cans sweat like matinee dancers
at the Platinum Cabaret
and it begins to sunshower.

Big Hands invites us in.
Russians mutely fuck on the television.

Richard unwraps his head—
what is left of his ear
is an uncased sausage.
Before I fix this up, how about a few lines
to get my head right? Like that, but thicker.
I press the asterisk

to find the hours of operation.
To set a wakeup call from the front desk.
The dial tone crinkles like swallowing tissue
paper in a dark room.
There is talk of a one-armed mechanic.
A cigarette on the devil's standtable.

Round Robin

I get back to wrestling
shape. My veins

fidget like worms
in the gymnasium light.

Balloons litter the rafters.
I fasten my headgear

and stretch
on the practice mats.

The routine
is a metal turnstile.

> *Shuck the*
> *wrists / control*
> *the space / keep / low don't*
> *drop / your*
> *head.*

I am the keystrokes

> of a courthouse stenographer.
>
> *Shuck the / wrists / control the space / keep / low don't drop / your head.*
>
> I scramble out of a rainbow cradle
>
> and ride his legs.
>
> Bodies fall around us like wet thunder.

Elegy for the Son of My Future Stepfather

I.

Handkerchiefs flitter in the reflective
lenses of sunglasses

the ex-wife wears indoors.
I feel like a clay pigeon.

A buzzcut in a letterman mimes grief
for comfort from the captain

of the gymnastics team—his crotch
a khaki pyramid.

I wait for my turn at the casket.
The vodka embrace

of my future stepfather
who found the boy

bluing from a tree in the yard.

II.

I thumbnail a stick family
into a Styrofoam cup

while my future stepfather
nips at an airplane

bottle. I make clouds
with my teeth.

They did a good job with his neck
don't you think?

Bring a Shovel to the Silo, the X Is North Ten Steps

I.

Remember the tree we built
a house in? How its arms would shadow
the shallow creek dividing tractors
from two-story families?
I went back to find it
sickened with the graffiti
of a younger generation.
I sawed its limbs off,
twisted them into a box.
It was empty, so empty, so
I placed our childhood in it.

II.

Dirty fingernails, I fashion
a crisscross of twigs
to mark the spot I buried it.
The moon is a white cocoon.
Young coyotes lick the warm air.
Like an anthill, the night
collapses into itself.

Winfield Township

Concrete mixers spin like music
box ballerinas. The afternoon
is a dead tooth. A still of smoke.
Children with eraser burns split
into separate armies
on the frozen lake.
The leader of each squad
situates himself in the dented cage
of a stolen shopping cart.
A sharp whistle
sends them headfirst.
Nearby, below the bison sanctuary,
atoms splinter inside the particle accelerator.
They bruise for bragging rights.
A kid with a crescent
gash on his forehead loses
consciousness in a snowbank
splotched with cat urine.

Water Scattering

When the gulls descend
a handful of men
tighten their newspapers

into baseball bats—
forearm veins pulsating
like suntanned rivers.

I toss my clementine skin
into the lake and find Richard
butterfly stretching near the courts.

He is up on me
love-thirty when an overhead serve
intercepts a low-flying bird. We converge

at the twitching resemblance
of its former architecture.
With my racket, I shovel

the limp starling
into a brown paper bag
and we proceed

to a nearby trashcan.
The cremation grows green
with the ink of discarded magazines.

Richard and I march
shoreward—fists upturned—
ashes trailing.

Caution: Doors Closing

The Green Line exhales
upon arrival.

I take a seat
in strange dampness

beside a beehive
hairdo with a cocoon-toothed
scar on her knuckle.

Yawns crisscross
the crowded aisle.

Blips of living
room television sets
run like water
behind a lullaby
of skulls.

I wake at the end
stop.
The wrong stop.
I get off.

The polluted sun
stretches the bridge's stiltbird
shadow. Tongues of wind

wet my eyelids.
Lakeshore traffic
slows
beneath the fireshower.

Yard Work

If I edge the yard,
so the woodchips
won't sneak out
of their beds,
will you reconsider?

With Crayons and Construction Paper

I follow her over the iron fence
into Oakland cemetery. Shoulder blades
against a headstone, she kicks
the blue jeans from her ankles.

Beyond the tangled-sway of her braids,
a purple-veined cumulonimbus begins to rise,
steady and deliberate as a palm
readying itself above a housefly.

When the sky splinters like a bridge of glass,
we gather ourselves under our elbows
and race the impending shatter
back to her front porch—four blocks west.

Out of breath, I duck inside my t-shirt
to light a cigarette. In the yard,
young trees bow like the necks
of horses crossing a finish line.

She tells me
our pupils are not black,
they are empty wells
the world falls into.

She tells me
this is what crying smells like.

Out of Picture in the City of Niceville

I lose my tattoo
virginity in a valley stitched
together with telephone wires.
Afterwards, the inkgun artist
tells me I am beautiful
as his dead brother.
On our calves, the grass
is damp and thin as the hair
of a newborn horse.
I swallow another muscle
relaxant.
Airships stall
in the artificial glow
above the greyhound track.

III

Dreamland

We order pitchers from the Twinkling Cow.
To go? To go.

Plasma donation center
hoppers ensemble, bandaged, near a firepit
in the gulch.

I hollow out
a lightbulb in an industrial tent.
The walls, they give a little.

A hawk clicks its sickle
beak against the baseball machine

like a glockenspiel.

The wind is
a milkshake
blender cup.

Richard unzips our sleeping

bags alongside swan boat river,
I make a pillow
out of my letterman jacket

as fireworks pock the peachfuzz
twilight above the miniature golf course

and the raccoons fuck like car horns
inside a clown mouth

funhouse of mirrors.
I wake to Richard yanking

out his eyelashes.
His gaze is animatronic

as we take turns with the shovel
and bury the firearm.

The Anarchist Cookbook

I pull a chair to the edge of the parade.
Snapdragons pepper the asphalt.
A stilted clown
guards the moonbounce entrance.
Its children a jumble of lottery balls.
A man in a paper hat
bathes Twinkies in a mobilized fryer.
The air machines hum.
Boys wade in a nearby retention pond.
A military GPS
specialist likens his desk job
to lawn darts
while he tongs sauerkraut.
I wheel around, dot my plate with deviled eggs
as the reigning harvest
queen rails lines in the backseat
of a Firebird
near the warning of a deaf child.

Air Traffic

I inch toward a bleeding
heron, all swiveling and unsure

on its orange leg.
Best to take a knee, make yourself
small as possible. No worries, here.
Little boy.
You can trust me.

I see razorblade
shadows when the lights are on.
Indoor eclipses perhaps.

Best to grab a fresh white towel.
Take the glass elevator to continental breakfast.

Think about the large metal trays
of eggs and Vermont flavored sausage—
warm drizzles of blueberry.

I won't tighten a belt
around the hotel doorknob.

I'll use it to hold up
my pants
like a businessman.

There is no one else on the boulevard.
Take a shovel
to the frozen yard.

Make a big fire.

Tuck me
in. Call me
your perfect little window garden.

Your Collapse Tastes Just Like Mine

Steel pylons chitter
like staple clicks
in the paralegal's cubic office.

If our suburb is a dream vandal,
someone has poured the concrete foundation
but it was us that spread the mulch
over a makeshift rabbit's grave.

Shrouded by azalea, we conspired
like patriots in unlit village tunnels—
a reverse mortgage was never an option
so we took a second one.

I bought a dog in your name.
No wonder he couldn't understand me.
My electric razor is a little lumbermill.
Touch my jaw. Tell it to stop grinding.

Lemon Windows

From my revolving office
chair, I measure
the western progress

of a sunflower minivan
with the width of an eyelash
I rescued from the bridge

of my nose—until a man
with white coveralls
and a squeegee

descends into vision.
Weeks later, we split an elevator.
His name is Ricardo.

He tells me
each window washer leaves
a unique signature.

He tells me
above the fortieth floor
the world is almost a silent one.

It Is Not My Birthday

Therefore, the package on my doorstep
surely contains some subhuman
infestation of nightmare:

a jumbled cloud of fire
ants or a cluster of autumn
skullcaps, perhaps a family

of mice—albino and foaming
with rabid intention.

It is January. Footprints
of delivery remain
undisturbed, lunar.

With a lobster claw
oven mitt I feed
the present into my fireplace

and listen
to the carbonation sizzle
of little souls

as they rise toward
the mouth
of my chimney

where they can at last
be exhaled into afterlife.

L Stop

I fight the word Mildew
in a softly lit pizzeria on the southside.
He is taller than expected.
Muscular even.
Bouquet of wiry hair.
Bowlegged. His sternum
a sunken ship. An indent
I could fit
a tongue in.

The Palace

The giant woman and I mount the projector
to watch a homemade montage
of milk
pouring in
extra slow motion.

I turn off the ceiling fan
and let the smoke meander—

rest my head on the soft hillside
of her stomach like a lumberjack trailing
off into a dark church.

On floorboards, I come to.
In my stash pocket,
a bulge
of piebald underwear.

Wednesday Before Last

Richard and I played
hot-potato with a hand mirror
in the conical glow

of a ceiling lamp. Teeth loose
with liquor I told him
about the nasogastric tube

in my father's stomach—
how scar tissue
has tightened like a fist

around his esophagus.
You have a Dad?
Lucky. Richard said, pressing

the lit end of his
cigarette into my forearm
like a punctuation.

It was my turn.
Richard lifted his earlobe,
offering the shallow valley

where jaw meets neck. Moths
circled us like soft moons.
Outside, the city was quiet

as a photograph.

The Routine

I remember most nights
like a skyscraper I am standing
across the street from—a peeled
orange pulsing in my palm—
the snowfall like telephone static.
Eclipsed by an orchid
growing limp on a second story
windowsill, a surgeon
tries to fit a lamb's cry
into five horizontal boxes.
Condensation rings bleed
into his Sunday newspaper.
One window over, a large man
crawls through a page
in the dictionary. If tomorrow
he can present his day camp
counselors with a new word,
he will be gifted a bouquet
of black licorice Twizzlers.
Farther up, a woman's tongue climbs
the varicose vines of her lover's thigh
while a spaghetti western
unspools in the VCR.
Wet floor signs inhabit
the otherwise vacant front desk
security monitors.
When the lobster shift
concierge's eyelids close
like manila envelopes,
I thread through the dwindling
lakeshore traffic toward
the lobby's warmth.

The Bus Is Late Again

I browse billboards
while Richard spits sunflower
seeds. Strings of saliva

solidify in his soul patch.
Pigeons congregate at his feet
like a town meeting.

The traffic light shifts
behind a cloud of fingerprints
left in grease

on the glass station wall.
An ambulance screams. I imagine
commuters thrown like popcorn

against the bus windshield.
Bystanders in business suits
swan diving into the wreckage—

armed with three hours of CPR training.
The fuel tank seeps
diesel onto the pavement. Like a snail

the pool crawls closer
to a tangle of fallen telephone
lines spitting electricity.

The Birthplace of Barbed Wire

I dress as the eyehole
of a skeleton, the unlit
hallways of a dollhouse

in storage, a spilt oil
butterfly on the concrete floor.
The garage door clicks

upward like a wooden
rollercoaster. The air
is a controlled prairie fire.

Flits of hair cross the moon
as I captain my wheelbarrow
past an apple tree

scaffolded with chicken wire.
I balance a bouquet
of planks on my shoulder

as flashlights
poke the fence slits
like the arms of a jailbird.

Candlestick Park

A tub of bacon-
wrapped asparagus in his lap,
the ornithologist
leans on the frayed arm
of a chair he could later die in.
A goose egg
in the bottom of the seventh.
The manager calls
for a left-handed closer.
Upstairs his daughter carves
a horse into her bedpost
with spaghetti fingers.
Unpaid hospital bills accumulate
on the answering machine like cat hair.
Look us up in the phonebook
or check your local newspaper.

Signal Transfer Malfunction

A knot of neighbors
with foreheads like rooftop satellite dishes

discuss the film of smog
swelling above our houses—

now thick as a mattress. Its arrival
coincided with internet connectivity issues

and county-wide cable outages.
Stalks of corn stand still as soldiers

in fields surrounding the subdivision.
A shortwave radio spits fuzz

from the shelf of an open garage.
Porch flags hang limp as dishrags.

A nearby radio tower pierces
the thickening—its blinking muffled.

Screams beneath a feather pillow.
The sky is birdless.

A family disappears
into the tinted stomach of an SUV.

The air smells of cough syrup.
Each living room on the cul-de-sac

is swaddled in television static—
the coalescence of their sets

left on at various volumes
sounds like a waterfall in the distance.

I have no intention of leaving.
This truth I hold close—

a calico kitten cupped against
the warmth of my chest.

The empty fifths on top of my refrigerator
rattle like cold teeth

when the first scribble
of lightning ignites the post office.

Petroleum Jelly Corset

A skeletal man blacks out
his left nipple for a more convincing
night sky. Bovine silhouettes

frozen in cones of alien light.
His navel is an artificial pond
speckled with koi

on the island of the cul-de-sac.
I shave a rectangle.
Dab isopropyl

on a ball of cotton.
The needle rattles along
like a model trainset.

In a metal spaceship
behind the schoolhouse

I nosh pickled nectarines
until my head

is a rhododendron.
We jiujitsu in the tall grass.

The Backwash of the Dead

for Matthew Schumacher

Insects scritch
in soybean stubble.
On a lost bet
you paw the detached
two-door for gasoline
canisters while I muffle
the omnipresent stench
of a cereal plant
with another stale cowboy
killer. Cystic acne
sandhills spew fire ants
in the pale stadium
between our headlamps.
We get high
off playing God
while the shapes
of our mothers shrink-
wrap funeral ham
above the granite island.
His breathing
machine in the corner
like a child
who refused to eat.
Man up, boy
he would say—
pointing at a plate
of cottage cheese.

A Half Glass

The ornithologist
jitters on the shower floor
like a carnival rollercoaster.

A prediagnosis
photograph of his daughter
above the baking soda

speckled mirror.
The warmth is waning.
Rivulets scroll down

his back like the end credits
of a drive-in double feature.
The towel rack is spent.

Naked, he spends whole
minutes in contemplation
of the hallway thermostat.

His throat
a distant car alarm.

Niceville

A woman with hair like a telephone
line full of birds
touched my face and asked me
to her place
for lobster ravioli.
Her laugh scratched
like the concrete underbellies
of public swimming pools.
I told her about
the television judge. After cinnamon
speckled tiramisu
she slipped me a kiss
and tightened my earmuffs.
The world grew
quiet and I learned to converse
with my fingers. They told me
I am no good.
They told me
she moved to a goat farm
in Vermont.

The sun tips
over like a giant egg.
I inhale
computer duster through a red straw.

IV

Panhandle

The bender continues.
Everclear and a pinch of tomato juice,
questionable ice cubes.
Big Hands scratches his elephant skull
as I apologize to the front desk lady for asking
her to bottomless oysters.
Richard snores in the armchair—
his ankle is a thundercloud.
I flip on the bathroom fan,

picture her on horseback in a garden
of telephone static
and jizz into the toilet bowl.
Ghouls in a wet tornado.

Outside, pigeons with volcanic
eyeballs pick at shreds of monkey bread
behind the pork shack.
I whistle about a rodeo clown

and punch secret numbers into the ATM
near the liquor barn.
The sky is a tangerine orchard.
In line, I split an airplane
shooter with my estranged uncle.

Richard and I Play with the Dead

the red tide has left us.
At his lips, the scooped eye of a fish

catches the starlight like a butterfly
knife opening a boy's palm.

A smoking pasture of hunched men
with zilch left to flutter

browse churro stands on the boardwalk.
The casino doors are guillotines.

The skyline is a hairless dog.
In our wake seagulls clatter like dented cans

strung to the exhaust pipe of a limousine—
its rear window: a shrinking rectangle.

A silhouette embrace. A sip of champagne.
A world map on a prison cell wall.

Equine Assisted Therapy

My first correspondence from outside
of here is a fingernail
crescent taped to a polaroid

of the giant woman with her eyes closed
in a velvet wingchair—
a fork held in her tangled cloud
of pubic hair.

Airstrip, I believe
is the formal term.

A garden
gnome near the projector.

The red wooden floor I left
my shoes on
after stumbling over.

The food slot clicks open like a mailbox.
Supper.

I picture a horse cock
growing hard
inside the refrigerator.

The predawn light
last October
above the municipal airport.

Leon County

In a cell without Richard
or a telephone
I taught myself to whistle
a song I call
Return to Cloud Book.

There are no bars to stick
my arms through.
Just a brown metal door.

The rhythm is a forehead
slowly coming open.
The taste of warm iron.

Vagrant Prophecy

I met a man with a beard
of orange leaves, his right eye
twitched like a sleeping dog.
He talked to me closely. He
warned me about the hand
in the sky. In preparation,
I spent years planting pencils,
thousands, into the divider island
of a major interstate. I clipped
my fingernails into shovels.
I survived off the kindness
of littering. In the rush
hours I went window to window
warning citizens. Soon,
I adopted a gasoline habit.
One night, I saw an adolescent deer
meet the grill of a white van
who hit and ran, left him there
wonky-legged and bleeding
in the road. I dragged him
to my island, whispered small prayers
into his ear and the stars
encircled us like a million
kneeling children. It was time.
I awoke in a forest of yellow
trees. When the air turned cold
they erased themselves.

Warning Label

The room smells of xylene. I want
to be an SUV
parked inside of the mall.

An explosion of red feathers
in a hospital.
I rehearse the number for Poison Control.

The guards switch out like ketchup
bottles on the table
of a diner not too far

from here. A man opens the sidewalk
with a jackhammer—
cigarette quaking in his mouth.

Satan or I
was an orphan.

With careful mirrors
they turn the prison into an aquarium.

When I First Met Richard

A colorless, noncorrosive, nontoxic gas. It is essentially odorless
with a barely perceptible sweet odor.
—United States Environmental Protection Agency

the sky was full of metal birds and his face
perspired like a carton of milk. I was rolling around

my portable Igloo, so he twisted me up a latex deer
for a can of cherry cola. The metropolitan park

was full of ice cream-
licking children with coinage to spare,

and I spent the rest of my sandwich watching
the magical arc of his fingers.

Once the sun retreated
behind the commercial rises

and the sugar cones were replaced by brown paper
bags, I invited Richard back to my apartment

to teach me how for twenty dollars. On our walk home,
the whispers of curious pedestrians echoed like shoes

in a museum. After carrying his metal tank
up three flights of stairs, Richard removed a heart-

shaped balloon and filled it with frozen air.
I touched my lips to his gloved fingers.

ACKNOWLEDGMENTS & NOTES

Above all, I would like to thank my goofy friends and family. I love you Mom, Dad, and Chloe. And, of course, my future wife Lindsey.

The poems in this book were inspired and encouraged by the following people: Patrick Balk, Anthony Blake, Nate Duke, Patrick Font, ZD Harrod, Brett Hanley, Zachary Hester, Lauren Howton, Josh Idaszak, Nancy Jureske, Scott Ray, Erin Slaughter, Casey Skufca, the University of Arkansas Program in Creative Writing & Translation, and the Florida State University Creative Writing Program.

I would also like to thank Geffrey Davis, Barbara Hamby, Michael Heffernan, James Kimbrell, David Kirby, and Davis McCombs for mentoring me.

I am grateful to the editors of the following publications, where some of these poems first appeared: *The Bitter Oleander; Blue Earth Review; Bat City Review; Carve Magazine; Cream City Review; Denver Quarterly; Forklift, Ohio; Gigantic Sequins; Granta; Grist; Hobart; Midwestern Gothic; Ninth Letter; Pleiades; Poetry Northwest; Seneca Review; SLICE;* and *Witness Magazine.*

"Thunderbird Inn" is dedicated to Denis Johnson.
"Your Collapse Tastes Just Like Mine" is a collaboration, written with Nate Duke.
"Songs Build Little Rooms in Time" owes its title to a lyric written by David Berman—to whom the poem is also dedicated.
"Dear Corporation" owes its title to the poetry collection *Dear Corporation* by Adam Fell.
"Coffin Rehearsal" owes its title to the song "Fatalist Palmistry" by Why?

An audio collaboration of the "The Backwash of the Dead" and "Vagrant Prophecy" was recorded, and later performed at open mics, with guitarist Collin McGee.

ABOUT THE AUTHOR

Collin Callahan was born in Illinois. His poems have appeared in *Granta, Pleiades, Denver Quarterly, SLICE, Hobart, Carve Magazine, Ninth Letter,* and elsewhere. He is the recipient of the 2021 *Bat City Review* Editors' Prize in Poetry. Collin is a graduate of the University of Arkansas and Florida State University. He currently lives and teaches in Tallahassee. You can find his work at collincallahanwrites.com.

OTHER TITLES FROM CONDUIT BOOKS & EPHEMERA

The Birthday of the Dead by Rachel Abramowitz
The World to Come by David Keplinger
Present Tense Complex by Suphil Lee Park
Sacrificial Metal by Esther Lee
The Miraculous, Sometimes by Meg Shevenock
The Last Note Becomes Its Listener by Jeffrey Morgan
Animul/Flame by Michelle Lewis